Christmas, 1776

By Brian J. Benjamin

Illustrated by Martin Wickstrom

The year was 1776.
America faced a crisis to fix.
British taxation without representation
angered Americans of every station.
They sought the freedom to make their own laws...
The right to liberty their sacred cause.

For Everett and Vivian

Christmas, 1776

ISBN: 979-8-9862514-0-0

American patriots took up their arms.
They left their homes, their shops, their farms.

These farm boys had grit, but little training.
The experience they lacked they would soon be gaining.

General George Washington would lead them to fight
Britain's oppressive imperial might.

George Washington was an American, born and bred.
Taller than most men by a head.

With 6 brothers, 3 sisters, he grew up strong.
The start of his adventures did not take long.

He joined the army at only twenty.
His triumphs and accolades came aplenty.

He fought in the French and Indian war,
and by the end he'd entered American lore.

Washington meets Seneca leader, Tanacharison the "Half King."

When the revolutionary war broke out,
America needed a leader no one could doubt.
They turned to their only living legend.
Barely another name was mentioned.
George Washington would lead them in this war,
to take on all the British had in store.

Second Continental Congress appoints George Washington
commander of the Continental Army, June 1775, Philadelphia.

They'd face British regulars skillfully taught,
perfectly disciplined before they fought.

The Brits had a few other friends they'd brought...
Some German soldiers whose support they'd bought.

And all these troops would cross the sea,
aboard the world's best Navy.

General Washington and his new army
prepared to defend New York City.
This coveted crown jewel of the colonies,
stood especially vulnerable to attack by sea.

The Americans worked to fortify their shore
before the Brits arrived to kick off the war.
The British came with 100 ships or more
and three times the men or maybe four.

The Americans tried to stand their ground,
but the British showed up and beat them sound.
From Long Island they were displaced...
From Manhattan they were quickly chased...
From the banks of the Hudson they were erased...
And into New Jersey they ran disgraced.

To the Delaware river they anxiously fled.
They crossed to safety but were filled with dread.

The war was less than two years old,
and the Americans were stranded in the cold.

Their greatest city, conquered, lost.
Their treasury wiped out by the cost.

Many Americans began to doubt
and feared they faced a certain rout.

The Brits pursued all the way to the river.
Then looked across and saw their enemies shiver.
With winter coming, December here,
the Redcoats felt they'd had a good year.
They retreated to conquered NYC,
to warm beds and Tory hospitality.
They left behind their German dogs of war
to guard the Delaware's Jersey shore.

With American hopes plainly fading
and British troops relaxing, celebrating,
Washington knew he must take bold action
for the Revolution to regain some traction.
He gathered his men to plan and plot
how to grab the victory they so desperately sought.

They decided on a holy night
to begin their brave and noble fight.

On Christmas night, they would embark
and cross the river in the dark...

Then march ten miles to surprise their foes,
and arrive to attack just as the sun rose.

Awaiting their final orders, the men held their breath.
George Washington stated gravely, "Victory or death."

With the plan all set, now just to wait.
They must keep the plan a secret and their heads on straight.
They braved a tense Christmas Eve and morn.
Then approached the ships on which they'd be borne.

In a light rain, General Washington crossed first.
The river was choppy with ice interspersed.
When the sun fell on that Christmas day,
the weather turned, and their plan gave way.

In an army with men of every station,
'twas the fishermen that rose to this occasion.
These expert sailors guided boat after boat
across nature's deadly, makeshift moat.
The rain had shifted to snow and hail,
but these brave men refused to fail.

They moved 2400 men across
and not a single soul was lost.
But the vicious weather had another cost...
Three hours against the plan were lost.

Finally, by four a.m. their march began,
and they braved the elements to a man.
They marched ten miles in hail and snow
to meet their skilled and rested foe.

They arrived well after the morning sun.
Not sure if by their lateness they'd been undone.

These brave men charged from the woods at a run,
and the German mercenaries were simply stunned.

How could an army arrive ready to fight,
after the terrible weather of the previous night?

General Washington led from the front on horseback and rebuffed every German counterattack.

American cannons fired with precision,
guided by Alexander Hamilton.

They raced through the town, took prisoners galore.
They shocked the mercenaries, pressing for more.
The Germans lost almost a thousand men.
The Americans lost less than ten.

After battling the weather all through the night,
it took less than an hour to finish the fight.

The next ten days were a complete whirlwind.
They crossed the river back and again.
First to deposit their captives and booty,
then returning to continue their tour of duty.

They stymied a British assault at Trenton.
Then launched a surprise attack at Princeton.
At Princeton, the famed British regulars were beat,
and the world was astounded by this colonial feat.

In the space of ten days, they'd secured two victories.
In the space of ten days, they'd changed the course of history.
On Christmas Eve, the American cause had been dead,
but now Britain was back on its heels instead.

The morale of the troops and colonists soared.
They again believed in what they were marching toward.
Towards life, liberty, and the pursuit of happiness,
to secure their rights and to crush British haughtiness.

America's birth was never a certainty,
but it was filled with men that would fight for it fervently.
These brave men volunteered to fight and die,
not knowing what their sacrifices might buy.

But we know the eventual success of their plan
and the day America's future began.
The day their deeds left the world transfixed...
Christmas, 1776.

Revolutionary War – April 1775 to August 1776 Major Political Events and Movements of George Washington's Continental Army

1. April 19, 1775 – Battles of Lexington and Concord. The "shot heard 'round the world" begins revolutionary war.
2. April 1775 – Patriot forces begin siege of Boston trapping British forces in the city.
3. May 10, 1775 – Second Continental Congress meets in Philadelphia.
4. June 14, 1775 – Congress creates continental army and names George Washington commanding general.
5. June 17, 1775 - Battle of Bunker Hill. British win tactical victory but are sobered by disproportionate casualties inflicted by Americans (1050 British casualties, 450 American casualties).
6. July 3, 1775 – Washington assumes command of Continental Army at Boston to continue siege.
7. March 4, 1776 - Continental army installs cannons overnight on Dorchester Heights overlooking city and harbor of Boston threatening British position.
8. March 17, 1776 – The British evacuate Boston by sea, Washington and Continental army retake city.
9. April 1776 – Continental army marches to New York City and begins to erect defenses awaiting British attack.
10. July 4, 1776 - Continental Congress ratifies the Declaration of Independence.

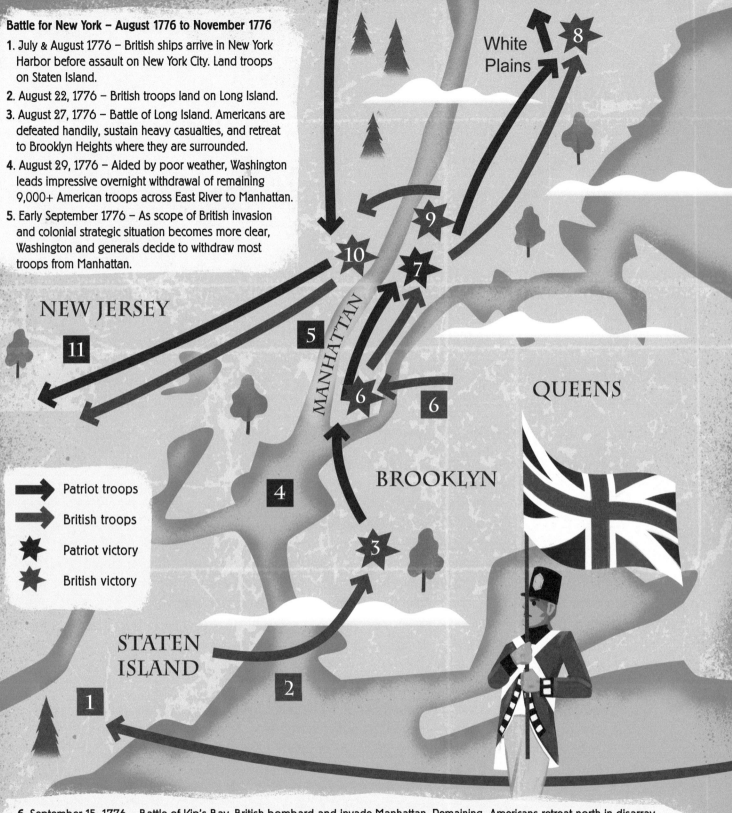

Battle for New York – August 1776 to November 1776

1. July & August 1776 – British ships arrive in New York Harbor before assault on New York City. Land troops on Staten Island.
2. August 22, 1776 – British troops land on Long Island.
3. August 27, 1776 – Battle of Long Island. Americans are defeated handily, sustain heavy casualties, and retreat to Brooklyn Heights where they are surrounded.
4. August 29, 1776 – Aided by poor weather, Washington leads impressive overnight withdrawal of remaining 9,000+ American troops across East River to Manhattan.
5. Early September 1776 – As scope of British invasion and colonial strategic situation becomes more clear, Washington and generals decide to withdraw most troops from Manhattan.

White Plains

NEW JERSEY

MANHATTAN

QUEENS

BROOKLYN

STATEN ISLAND

Patriot troops
British troops
Patriot victory
British victory

6. September 15, 1776 – Battle of Kip's Bay. British bombard and invade Manhattan. Remaining Americans retreat north in disarray.
7. September 16, 1776 – Battle of Harlem Heights. Washington leads reformed continental army in small victory over British. It serves as an important morale boost for the Americans.
8. October 28, 1776 – Battle of White Plains. British pursue continental army retreating north and win battle of White Plains. Washington forced to retreat even further north of city eventually crossing Hudson at Peekskill.
9. November 16, 1776 – Battle of Fort Washington. British take fort on Hudson River. Crushing defeat for Americans as over 2,800 continental soldiers are taken prisoner.
10. November 20, 1776 – Battle of Fort Lee. British successfully cross Hudson into New Jersey. Washington orders complete evacuation of Fort Lee.
11. November 20 – December 6, 1776 – Retreat across New Jersey. Washington leads the continental army in a retreat across the entire state of New Jersey. The army crossed the Delaware river into Pennsylvania near Trenton.

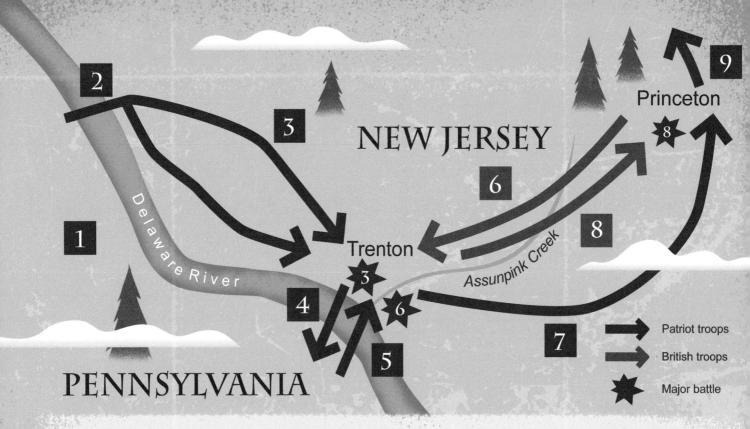

Ten Crucial Days: Americans Counterattack – December 25, 1776 to January 3, 1777

1. Early to Mid December 1776 - Washington and Generals plan Delaware crossing. Round up boats and barges up and down Delaware river.

2. December 25, 1776 - Washington and 2400 men begin crossing the Delaware river in the evening. The weather turns horrible: rain, sleet, hail, snow. The crossing is not completed until 3am on the 26th.

3. December 26, 1776 - Battle of Trenton. After river crossing, continental army splits into 2 columns and marches nine miles to Trenton. The 2 columns arrive and attack simultaneously taking German/Hessian mercenaries completely by surprise and win a convincing victory. Germans lost ≈ 100 killed and or wounded and almost 900 captured. Americans had less than 10 total casualties.

4. December 26, 1776 - Washington and men cross Delaware again back into Pennsylvania this time bringing their 900 prisoners and all of the captured supplies from the battle.

5. December 30, 1776 - Washington and his army cross back over the Delaware and take up defensive positions on the south side of Assunpink creek south of Trenton.

6. January 2, 1777 - Battle of Assunpink Creek. After being harassed all day by American troops as they marched across New Jersey, British General Cornwallis and his troops arrive at Assunpink creek in the evening. They attempt 3 charges over the creek's only bridge but are repulsed each time by American fire. British army retires for the night with the plan to attack again in the morning.

7. Night of January 2-3, 1777 - Washington and continental army stealthily withdraw overnight and take back roads to Princeton with plans to launch surprise attack against British forces there.

8. January 3, 1777 - Battle of Princeton. American troops arrived in the morning again achieving the element of surprise and gaining a convincing victory inflicting disproportionate British casualties and capturing 300 British soldiers. Cornwallis pursues that morning, but too late to stop American win.

9. January 1777 - After the battle, Washington and his army march to Morristown, New Jersey and set up their winter quarters. British General Cornwallis and the British army abandon most of New Jersey and return to New York City for the winter. The victories at Trenton and Princeton provided a huge morale boost to the American cause and lead to a surge of enlistments in the spring making sure the American cause survived another year.

About the author
Brian J. Benjamin

Brian J. Benjamin may be a chemical engineer by
training, but he has a love of American history and
a compulsion to make everything rhyme that
he's combined to write his first children's book.
He hopes this book will spark an interest in
American history for all the children that come across it.

He'd love if you visited
brianJbenjamin.com
to find out how to hear about
future books he's working on.

About the illustrator
Martin Wickstrom

Sweden born illustrator Martin Wickstrom lives
and works in New Jersey, U.S.

For any inquiries about his work, please visit
WickIllustration.com
or
IllustrationOnline.com.

Made in United States
Troutdale, OR
11/21/2024

25151029R00021